The Wurlitzer
and other Poems

DOMINIC HYLAND

THE CHOIR PRESS

Copyright © 2024 Dominic Hyland

All rights reserved. No part of this publication may be reproduced or transmitted in any form or by any means, electronic or mechanical including photocopying, recording or any information storage or retrieval system, without prior permission in writing from the publishers.

The right of Dominic Hyland to be identified as the author of this work has been asserted by him in accordance with the Copyright, Designs and Patents Act 1988

First published in the United Kingdom in 2024 by
The Choir Press

ISBN 978-1-78963-432-7

To my family

Contents

The Wurlitzer	1
A Marathon Fantasy	3
Christmas Present	6
Corona Pop	8
How Do I love You?	9
In Praise of Christmas Cards	10
My Hair Prayer	11
Inkerman Street	12
New Year Poem (2023)	13
Parting is not Sweet Sorrow	14
The Joy Of Giving	15
Dog Growl	16
Reality Bites	18
My Calendar Girl	19
Matinee Idol	20
Christmas Greetings	21
You haven't a leg to stand on	23
My Valentine	28
The Highs and Lows of Love	29
Winter Woolies	31
Missing Kissing … A Poem for Covid Times	32
Be My Love	33
Have a Meaningful Christmas	34
Valentine	36
She is not fair to outward view	37
It's Christmas Again	39
Trying Trials in Times of Torment	40
Peace in Our Time	42
A Christmas Invitation (2003)	43

Feet First	45
Repent At Leisure	46
Friendship	48
L'Amour	49
I Remember …	50
A Christmas Sceptic	54
Victory In Europe	55
Away In A Manger	56
Christmas	58
Twenty Twenty Two	59
Le Mariage	61
"Come live with me and be my love"	64
November	65
Ode To 'Alifax	66
Christmas 2018	69
Rain Stopped Play	70
Your Valentine	71
I Love You	73
When we are old and grey and full of sleep	74
You Are Lovely	75
Advice on The Onset of Old Age	76
Christmas Din Din	77
Boy Meets Girl	78
Victorian Values	79
The End of Friendship	81
The LFC Victory Parade	82
When I'm Gone … An Obituary Piece	83

The Wurlitzer

Outside the sun is glinting
On the Blackpool esplanade.
The golden sands are filled with kids
Armed with bucket and with spade.
The sea seems so inviting
The boats bobble in the bay.
So, why am I not outside
On such a lovely day?

The secret is that I'm in love
With the world of dance and music.
The dazzle of the strobe lighting
The hint of musk and magic.
The swish of skirt, the subtle hint
Of hips and glimpse of stocking
Is what I long for on a Saturday.
I don't think that's too shocking!

It was on just such a summer's day
That I met this wondrous girl,
She chose me in an 'excuse me'
And set me in a whirl.
She swept me off my feet
She raised me to the heights,
Everything was just a blur
Under the ballroom lights.

I realised that here was love's true dream
The reason I was there,
As she wrapped her arms around me
We were Ginger and Astaire.
The love I felt was all too much
'Twas more than I could bear,
As we twirled around the ballroom floor
I thought, in one whirl – it's her!

A Marathon Fantasy

Who's that up ahead?
She's a bit of a stunner.
Thank goodness I decided to try being a runner!
It seems only minutes
Since she flew past me last.
I didn't think girls could travel that fast!

She seems on a mission – it's called 'OVERTAKE'
And simply leaves everyone else in her wake.

Mind you, though, she has a shapely silhouette.
So I think I'll speed up a little
And hope to get
A better view of what she's wearing.
It's all quite exciting, I feel so daring.

Oops! Wait a minute,
Is she wearing Nike, the goddess of Victory?
Now that's what I like:
A girl who obviously has high aspirations
Who never breaks sweat – it's perspiration.

Come on, concentrate
She is getting away,
She's not going to wait,
She's not got all day.

Give up, you've no chance
You'll never get near her.
Just accept, after all,
You are just an outsider.

I guess she has run lots of marathons before
And has proved to be a natural winner.
But look at me... hopeless
Just a beginner.

O look out! I have lost her
She'll lap me again.
She's running as though
She'll be late for a train.

Hello. What is happening?
Someone's pushed me aside.
He is running alongside her.
Stride matching stride.

Get lost! You big bounder!
Move aside, run around her.
I saw her first, don't try muscling in
You're here for the sport, you came here to win.
Just cos you've got all those muscles
All over the place,
Remember your priority
Lies in the race!!

But now, where's she gone?
She has just disappeared!
Surely not with the hunk- just as I feared.
I guess she was really well out of my league
And, I have to admit: after only five miles
There's already a threat of rotten fatigue.

Ah well, *c'est la vie*, as we know Frenchies say,
With their usual *sang froid*.
But between you and *moi*, you never can tell,
If I joined a French marathon
I may meet a mademoiselle.

Christmas Present

The Chosen People, for thousands of years
Had waited impatiently for the Messiah to appear
And yet they really had no idea
What he'd be like.

They seemed convinced he'd be a king
With power and majesty and everything
That would set them free and make them rich
And rid them of anything which
Might do them harm.

They insisted he'd be like their great King David,
Indeed, he must be David's heir!
He'd be a warrior, a conqueror,
He'd spread his kingdom everywhere,
He'd be more like a whirlwind than a breeze,
His enemies, subjected, would bend their knees
In base submission, trembling with fear.

Imagine, then, just how they felt
When Christ appeared on earth.
Instead of a noble palace
A shed was his place of birth.
There were no noble courtiers
Drenched in rich perfume
Instead there were sheep and cattle
Crowded into a stinking room.
And his parents were Galilean Nazarenes
Who were held in gross contempt
Is this what God had promised?
This could not be what he meant!

Yet we Christians are so proud
To sing our carols and shout out loud
That this is what gives life its worth
That this indeed is God on earth.

HAPPY CHRISTMAS

Corona Pop

Suddenly the world turns dark
As when Noah built his ark.
But he was only troubled by water
Covid19 is another matter.
You cannot see it, or touch it, or smell it
But it can see you off if you're old or debillit-
ated- You'll be in bits like that last word!
It came from nowhere, though I have heard
That China is to blame- Death: Made in China-
But it soon spread world-wide and played a blinder
Against Italy especially, and now it's in England.
It has only just reached us but when will it end?
It's wreaking havoc but especially for lovers
Who may lose one another until it is over!
But if their love is strong and sincere and secure
They'll be back in each other's arms once more.

How do I love you?

How do I love you? Let me count the ways.
I love the way your presence can
Change dark nights into days.

I love the way that your smile can
Light up every face.
I love the way in one short while
I am warmed by your embrace.

I love the way you make me feel
Important, loved, and treasured.
I love you with a depth of love
That, simply, cannot be measured.

I love the stories that you tell
I love their joy and laughter,
I love to think of hearing them
And our living happily ever after.

In Praise of Christmas Cards

"Don't send Christmas Cards" they say,
"Give the money to charity."
Great idea, you may agree.
But we can't escape the mystery
Of Christmas on a single-coloured card
Which, I have to say, we send out by the yard
Despite the warning (quite well meant)
Of harm to the environment.
For Christmas is a time of hope not warning,
It tells of a new life dawning.
It gives us, too, as this year ends
The chance to contact distant friends,
In a small way to make amends
For neglecting them since last year!
A Christmas card helps bring them near.

My Hair Prayer

Dear Lord, can you make my hair apparent?
I used to have lots but now I haven't !
It was lovely and curly and gorgeously black
And all that my prayer is : "Please give it me back!"
Don't worry about the colour – no doubt it should be grey –
"Beggars can't be choosers" is what they say.
I know that hair loss can be just natural wastage
And it occurs, I believe, with the advancing of age.
But I do feel it's something of an unfair disadvantage.
It's not exactly kind and does call into question
Your sense of justice and abuse of divine intervention.
Indeed, one story that's found in that book that you wrote
Tells of the distress of one hero of note,
Samson by name who, according to the story,
Was deprived by his girlfriend of his own crowning glory!
It robbed Samson immediately of his strength and sex appeal
And I certainly can relate to how that made the poor man feel!
Now, there are lots of other tales in your book that I read,
Stories of wonders like bringing back people from the dead.
All I am asking is for a few hairs on my head!
I've a great supply of combs and brushes and oodles of shampoo,
All I am missing, Lord, is some hair-raising action from you.
                        Amen

Inkerman Street

Come live with me and be my love
We've known each other now for years.
It seems so pointless to live apart
We spend so much on those bus fares.

Your mum and mine will be all right,
They've got their tellies and their phones.
They can come to us on Sundays
It's not a long ride home.

I've found this house on Inkerman Street
Not too far from the docks.
It's got a lovely garden
Full of dandelion clocks.

There's a Kwik Save and a chippy near
So we'll have lots to eat.
There's a bookies on the corner, too,
It's a dandy little street.

We've got our bits and pieces,
They'll look nice upon the shelf.
I love your little knick-knacks
And you're rather nice yourself.

So come with me and be my love,
Our house will be a treasure-trove
But the most precious treasure of them all
Will be life with you my love.

New Year Poem (2023)

I have put away last year's calendar,
With mixed feelings it must be said,
Because it's like losing a friend who was very dear
And you're burying the dead!
So, before I put it in a drawer I studied all the pages
To remind me of the fun we've had at all the different stages
Of 2022, a year I will always treasure,
A year full of delights and every kind of pleasure.
LFC had won two cups – that's something seldom seen! –
Graham had married Denise, Clara had reached eighteen!
I had had my dose of Covid, I had holidayed in Wales,
I had had my 87th birthday, I was ten stone on the scales!
The calendar is full of lovely photographs in brilliant
    technicolour,
And I hope that the one in 2023 can be even better.
So here's looking forward to all that this year brings,
May all my friends be happy friends and enjoy the best life
    brings.

Parting is not Sweet Sorrow

I'll tell you how it feels
When we have to part:
It feels as though
I've blown a hole in my heart!
I hate that moment
When we go our own ways.
And I start to wonder:
How many days
Might it be till we meet again?
The days in between can be so full of pain.
It may sound maudlin,
It may sound immature,
But whatever it is
Of this I am sure:
I'm so happy that we came together once more.

The Joy of Giving

(a thank you for the gifts of flowers, grapes and water)

Human beings are so rightly proud of their wonderful inventions:
Of planes that fly across the sky in all manner of directions,
Of phones that can help us talk across the seas and mighty oceans,
Of the miracle of medicines and life-saving operations,
Of the beauty that is music in all its variations,
Of the power of Art in all its forms and magnificent depictions,
Of so many geniuses in every land and nation.

Yet, in addition to all of this, we must stand in awe
Of the beauties that come from the natural law
Created by the Almighty who set up a store
Of colour, of scents, and of shapes and of power,
The abundance of fruits and the magic of flowers.
And, what can be said of the wonder of water?
That generous gift of a generous Creator
Who gave us the Sea, the Waterfall, and the River
All wonderful gifts of a wonderful Giver.

Dog Growl

Some people say I'm a bit of a woofian.
I have to admit I am a toughie, an'
Of all the dogs mine is the loudest bark,
I know Noah would not allow me in his Ark!
My little friend, George, is such a sweetie
You'd never refuse him any treat, he
Is so well behaved and he doesn't bite
He sits up and begs – he is so polite!
With one of the dogs, I'm going steady,
He's only tiny and they call him Teddy.
But there's no future in it, as I'm sure he knows,
There is so little space between his tail and his nose!
Betty, by far, is my favourite playmate,
We met in the park and she was my first date.
We romped and we wrestled, we ran and we scampered,
If she lived with me she'd be so spoiled and so pampered.
Simon's dog, Max, is the quietest of them all,
He's gorgeous in colour and stands proud and tall,
He stays close to his master, close to his side,
And, though Simon has a scooter, Max never asks for a ride.
Two other friends, Mia and Lucy,
Come as a pair because, you see,
They belong to Helen who set up this party.
But, of course, you won't see me or Lucy or Mia,
Cos dogs aren't allowed to come in here.
In contrast to Helen, two fellas have Bella,
One of them is Tom, the other is Alex,
Both think of themselves as the best of dog whisperers,
And Bella's behaviour shows that they are true masters!
Sam is the dog who arrives here in style
I think he lives close – certainly well under a mile,-

He arrives in his limo, and then struts his stuff
He looks such a softie but he can be quite tough.
Eric's big dog puts us all in the shade,
His master's the man who comes armed with a spade,
It's not that Jackson creates lots of poo
It's just that our Eric likes something to do.
Miri and Alfie, now they're a fine pair
They may have joined late but now that they're here
They join in the fun and Miri brings lots of treats,
Miri's the type of girl that I like to meet!
Now, it would surely be the height of folly
If I omitted to mention Fiona and Molly.
They are both so quiet, polite and serene
The opposite of me, you know what I mean.
Barbara's dog, Sweep, is a sweet Shiatzu poodle
And she is the last in my little doodle.
She has gorgeous, curly, raven-black hair,
I intend to be seeing a lot of her!
"Sweep…I'm coming!!"

*Bye, bye…Robyn*xxxx

Reality Bites

Jealousy means that you feel insecure.
Jealousy means that you're never quite sure.
Once in its grip you are never at ease,
And it lingers and spreads like a malignant disease.
You've become so dependent on your lover's affections
That the threat of its loss spreads like an infection
Which can run out of control and drive you insane
For fear that you may never see your lover again.
There is no easy cure…indeed no cure at all!
Avoid falling in love, just be superficial.
Have fun while it lasts, just live for the present,
Establish ground rules by mutual consent.
It may sound cold-hearted , and not very nice,
But take it from me: it's quite sound advice.
If all else fails just submit to defeat,
Be brave and admit you cannot compete.
Why suffer those pangs that tear you apart?
Take care of yourself, take care of your heart.

My Calendar Girl

Pinups come in all shapes and sizes
And finish up on all kinds of wall.
What comes to me as no surprise is
That none of these appeal at all.
There is no need for shapely parts:
The narrow hips, the panting bosom.
What we men need, in our heart of hearts,
Is a loving smile and a loving woman.
That's not to say that the total package
Might not include the extra bits,
But remember the words of the ancient adage
"Before you buy make sure it fits."
And so, you see, my Calendar Girl
Is not a model for lingerie,
But someone who's the centre of my world
I'm made for her and she's made for me.
It comes, then, as no surprise at all
That the pin-up on my special wall
Is a picture of me with a beaming smile
Next to an angel walking down the aisle.

Matinee Idol

He saw himself as Clark Gable in Gone with the Wind
Or as Douglas Fairbanks Jr. sailing on the Golden Hind.
When he looked into the mirror he saw the clean-cut jaw,
The hero who fought for justice and came back for more.
He dreamed of daring-dos,
Of rescuing fair maidens,
Of swashbuckling on the high seas,
Of pirates and dark dungeons,
Of scaling castle walls and parapets,
Or, armed with sword and shield
Crying, "Hold you heinous villain
Yield, you coward, yield."
He searched the seas for sunken treasure,
Scaled mountain tops and peaks,
Braved storms and avalanches,
Crossed the desert's sandy wastes,
Like Greg Peck or Gary Cooper
In life's unending quests.

But all those stars of the silver screen,
The countless stars of films he'd seen,
The Tyrone Powers and Victor Matures
Surrounded by their paramours
Who'd been at the Gaumont or the Odeon
The Trocadero or Palladium,
Came to an end in Wigan one time
When he met his Valentino in the one and nine's
And surrendered to his Valentine.

Christmas Greetings

The cards come tumbling through the door
One after one, and well before
You've even thought of sending yours!

But isn't it nice for us to know
That, at least at Christmas,
People go to such great lengths
Simply to say
'I love you so'?

And that's the main and touching reason
For us to celebrate this lovely season
When Love came down as our free gift.

Love wasn't wrapped in tinsel or bows
But cast-off, make-shift swaddling clothes.
No sweet-smelling perfumes in a stable
For, on that wintry, star-lit night
Mary was barely able
To keep Him warm.

The spirit that gave us Christmas day
Must stay with us each and every day
Throughout the year
Or else:
What is He doing here?

You haven't a leg to stand on

'Twas on the Night of Mischief in the year 2006
When poor, defenceless Dominic, was simply hit for six.
As the rain drizzled through the eerie neon lights
It would prove to be the most dismal of dismal Scouser nights.
Poor Dominic until that time had had a lovely day,
And everything, simply everything, had been going all his way.
The evening saw the clash of Liverpool and Bordeaux
With LFC the victors as everybody knows (3 – 0).
Dear Dominic, elated, was stepping merrily along,
With a spring in his step, his heart full of song.
Walton Road (the main road) was chock full of traffic
And Dominic, ever watchful, had to be alert and quick.
As he crossed one side-road all seemed to be clear
But a reckless, careless driver, suddenly cost him dear.
Just halfway across this empty street
It came as a shock for him to meet
A dark blue Vauxhall Vectra whose bumper he saw
Strike his knee and dump him helplessly on the floor.
For a moment or two Dominic thought that all was well.
Until he tried standing up but his knee gave him hell.
It simply collapsed and gave no support.
The accident was more serious than Dominic had thought.
He crawled to the kerb and found help close at hand
In the form of some Scousers who had heard the big bang.
They held Dominic up and provided a chair
From a pub on the corner, and it was from there
That they phoned the police and the ambulance, too,
And tried to make a note of the driver who
Had switched off his lights and fled from the scene.

An act that was cowardly, cold, and obscene.
The ambulance came and drove into the night
Till Fazakerley Hospital hove into sight.
A sprawling great fortress twelve storeys high,
Obscuring the sun, defacing the sky.
A looming grey edifice uninviting and dim
The endless green corridors seemed equally grim.
But the staff seemed efficient, the Bobbies were kind,
The X-rays were taken, and Dominic expected to find
Himself speeding homeward leaving Anfield behind.
But fate did not smile kindly on this LFC fan,
And that night of November the nightmare began.

A trolley was ordered and they wheeled Dominic along
Green, dimly-lit corridors where all, old and young,
Lay fitfully sleeping, tossing, groaning, distressed,
Desperately seeking precious moments of rest.
Dom could not envisage what lay then in store
As the lift climbed relentlessly to the seventh floor,
And Ward 17 a five-bedded bay
Where Dominic was deposited and awaited the day.

The hospital day starts at 6.30 prompt,
Your blood pressure's taken, your body is pumped,
Pummelled, heaved, and well fed,
For the first time in years
Dominic had breakfast in bed.
But don't think of sausages, fried bacon and egg, instead
Think of porridge or cereals and slightly stale bread.
As the milk and the crumbs tumbled down on his chest
Dominic surveyed the scene of other poor wrecks
Poor adverts indeed for our proud male sex.

In one corner lay a mound of a man
Whose simple ambition was to fill a bed pan.
Gone indeed were the dreams he had as a youth:
To seek out adventure, joust for the truth,
Win the hand of a maiden, sail the high seas.
All these count as nothing compared to the ease
He prayed for as he lay there prostrate
Knowing nothing would move whatever he ate!
Tiny Tim admitted to being eighteen stone
But I am sure that that measure had long since gone.
He needed a hoist to use the bed pan
Which, at the end, stood as empty as when he began.
Poor Tim had broken his thigh in three places,
And he dreaded the times he was put through his paces
By two slips of a girl called Angie and Sarah
The Fazakerley physios who were a pair o'
Amazons fit for the fray and ready to go.
To Tim they were known as the Fazakerley Gestapo.
The curtains were drawn, the groaning began.
There's nothing quite like a groaning eighteen-stone man.
Tim's well over eighty and the last time I heard
Is that Tim had been moved to a sound-proofed ward.

In another far corner lay another sad case:
A man in his 30s who was quite out of place.
Dear Peter's autistic and had been born with no eyes
And, like Tim, Peter was of a significant size.
On strong medication he writhed and he twisted
Though, strong as he was, he never resisted
When staff came to help him and feed him and such
He reacted quite well to a soft voice and touch.
He ate all he was given, had a fondness for tea,
Had an ear for good music and Radio Three.

But, once darkness fell, Peter gave us a fright
As he slipped out of bed in the middle of the night.
With an uncanny instinct some blind people show
He would seek out for attention the one person who
That day had had treatment on an arm or a leg,
And drag them, protesting, from the warmth of their bed!
Dear Peter, one must say, intended no harm
Though his nightly excursions did cause some alarm!
Disturbed by the chemicals at large in his system
It's no wonder he caused panic, havoc and mayhem.
On occasion, the hospital put someone on vigil,
But somehow our Peter knew that at some point the guard will
Fall asleep, take a break, and help out with a patient
And that, for dear Peter, seemed the opportune moment.
There were howls and commotion, the ward's silence was fractured,
No one could feel safe until Peter was captured.
An executive decision was finally taken,
And poor Peter was moved to a different location.

However, my final escape was not so easy.
The O.T. Department said it felt rather queasy
That my toilet at home had no proper prop
And, until one was purchased, I just had to stop-
Not going to the toilet, of course, that's just silly,
Stop where I was, they meant, you silly billy!
The piece of the jigsaw that was still missing
Was a frame round the toilet to help me, when sitting
And needing to rise without any assistance
That was the focus now of their insistence.
They had none in stock, which meant four days' delay
And NHS patients cost £500 a day.

So Clare bought a frail frame for 45 quid
And I guess that the tax payer was glad that she did.
So, on Friday the 10th, before Armistice Day,
A wobbly Dominic was sent on his way,
Without copies of X-Rays or scans or a script
He was wheeled unceremoniously as far as the exit.
No ambulance waited at the hospital door-
Due notice was needed four days before.
But Jenny, our neighbour, gave me a lift
Stretched out on the backseat of her VW Passat.
Her wonderful kindness spared me a long stay
In a hell of a hospital a nightmare away.
Nannette, who had visited me day in and day out,
Held my hand as Jenny drove away from the Scouse.
'Twas not the leaving of Liverpool that grieved me
'Twas the coming home to Thornton that relieved me!

My Valentine

Valerie was a luscious dish
Angela met my every wish
Lydia had a generous smile
Eliza simply drove me wild
Natalie had that gentle touch
Tina – well – she was – aw – so much!
Imogen was a trophy on my arm
Naomi had such grace and charm
Emily lavished me with kisses.
But the moral of all of this is:
Woman is man's joy and all his bliss!
And the girl I cherish and adore
Has all these qualities – and more!

The Highs and Lows of Love

In love affairs it's good advice
To guard against extremes.
Thus, for example, old men shouldn't date
Young women in their teens.
And women of a certain age
Should steer clear of youths in jeans.
Make sure that, when you stand upright,
You remain aware of each other's height
Too much disparity in size
Makes it difficult to gaze into each other's eyes!

But in my present story
Two lovers took a risk,
For she was all of six-foot-two
And he was just a titch.
So, when they went out courting
And went smiling through the town,
He was forever looking up
And she was looking down.

Her nickname for him was Tiny
His name for her was Val,
He not only loved her with all his heart
But saw her as his best pal.
They shared everything together,
Summer hols and fish and chips.
There was nothing he liked better
Than salt and vinegar on her lips.

They saw themselves as bride and groom
They started making preparations:
Booking cars, hotel and bedroom
Informing their relations,
Hiring dinner suits, buying trousseaux,
Wedding rings and all those presents,
Checking menus, booking discos –
Time was of the essence.

The wedding day dawned bright and clear,
The chapel bells were ringing.
The sun shone bright on the bride in white
And the choir was sweetly singing.
The minister pronounced them man and wife:
"She is yours and he is thine,
You may kiss each other now you're wed.
You've done it Val 'n' Tine!!"

Winter Woolies

I thought you would welcome a little something
To keep you warm on a Norfolk night
When the air is cold and you're out of kindling
And the wind is howling with all its might.
Gone are the balmy days of summer,
Gone are the blue skies and any warm glow.
Grey skies and rain – what a bummer-
Are all we'll expect as far as we know.
So, if all that happens – and we hope it won't—
Wrap up warm and be nice and cuddly.
Spoil yourself (you usually don't),
Help yourself to a glass of bubbly.
Enjoy every moment – that's the point!

Missing Kissing ... A Poem for Covid Times

Kissing for me comes top of the list,
You've never known Kindness if you've never been kissed.
And by kissing I mean the full strength of emotion,
The kiss sets the seal on a lover's devotion.
It starts from the heart and is expressed by the lips,
It travels quite rapidly down to the hips.
It sets stirring within you strong waves of desire,
It makes your whole being aflame, full of fire!
So, if you want to show love, try kissing for sure.
It won't be refused, people come back for more.
And, by kissing, I don't mean a peck on the cheek:
The kisses I mean are not for the meek!
xxxxxx

Be My Love

One day without your lovely smile
Means the world's a bitter place.
A barren landscape no longer lit
By the beauty of your face.

Your laughter is a thousand songs
Played to the sweetest tunes.
A melody that breathes delight
More real than rich perfumes.

I love to feel your warm embrace
The closeness of your touch,
The look of love, the words that say
"I love you so very much."

So, never let a day pass by
Without your being mine
To love, to hold, to kiss and say:
"You are forever mine."

Have a Meaningful Christmas

They say it didn't happen
Like the Gospel writer said,
That there were no signs and angels,
That he meant something else instead.
The shepherds didn't greet Our Lord
In a manger for his bed.

They say the story's just a myth,
A legend handed down
In ancient times, in many tongues,
As men moved from town to town.

Have they lost their sense of wonder
Of surprise and sense of awe?
Is there no place for dreams and visions
Or such marvels any more?
Unless we see such things ourselves
Do we reject what others saw?

Believers know that Christ was born
To show us how to love,
To make some sense of mystery,
To show us how to move
Beyond our merely mortal grasp
Of what we hear and feel.
To show a world he knew of
And to make it real.

So, have a lovely Christmas,
May all your joys increase.
May you find that life is a wondrous thing
Made by the Prince of Peace.

The winter's nearly over
And spring is on its way
The daffodils and crocuses
Are beginning to have their say,

My love! You mean so much to me
You ARE my Valentine.

Valentine

The winter's nearly over
And spring is on its way,
The daffodils and crocuses
Are beginning to have their say.

So it seems only fitting
As the sun begins to shine,
That I should send this wish to you:
Please be my Valentine.

Your love will bring the warmth again,
Your kisses bring the wine.
The year will have more meaning
If you'd be my Valentine.

I see you smiling brightly,
There's a sparkle in your eyes.
These signals mean so much to me
Of a promise to be mine.

You've put your arms around me
Your lips are close to mine.
My love! You mean so much to me
You ARE my Valentine.

She is not fair to outward view

She is not fair to outward view.
Though she's better than many
And I've known a few!

She's a heart of gold
And a brain like Einstein,
Legs like Gable
And both are mine.

So, I'm as proud as punch
When we walk arm in arm,
Though I have to admit
Her face causes alarm.
I think it's the eyes
As they roll in her face
Following people round
At a terrible pace.

She's got the voice of an angel
But it's on Judgement Day.
Not so much melodic
But a trumpet's bray.
When she holds me close
In a loving clinch,
I have to confess
To the hint of a flinch.
And the force of her kiss
Almost sucks my teeth out.
She loves a good kiss
Of that there's no doubt!

So, though she's no Madonna
Or Kylie Minogue,
And never wears clothes
Remotely in vogue,
She's the girl that I love
And I know she loves me
Moreover ... I'm eighty
And she's twenty-three!

It's Christmas Again

To think: a whole year has passed
And winter's come with its rain and blasts.
And the eyes have lost a little more sparkle
And the ears can't pick up those little crackles
And we rarely think now of a slap or a tickle!
And the bones tend to creak,
And have lost part of their function.
And one of our pleasures
Is applying the unction
That helps ease our pain and encourages motion!
We are getting older and people are talking
About the trouble we have when we are walking.
And people offer us seats on trains and buses
And we ourselves wonder what all the fuss is.
And yet, at Christmas, old people's homes' denizens
Suddenly feel like super citizens:
There is spring in their step
Fat people feel slimmer
No need for a stick or the everyday zimmer.
It is the season of hope,
It's the season of cheer.
It's the season of joy
For Christmas is here.

Trying Trials in Times of Torment

This is not the threat of the Grim Reaper.
At least we recognised him armed with his scythe.
His intention was blatant
No attempt at disguise.
And there is no escape from that ruthless killer
He just sweeps you away.
You might run, try to hide, you may plead for mercy
But he is the Grim Reaper and you die anyway.
Yet he might give you some warning
He might give you a chance:
"I am the Grim Reaper
Care for a dance?"

And with the Angel of Death,
You may well remember,
You were possibly spared
If you were a member
Of the Jewish community
And had blood to hand
And could smear it on door posts
Password?: Promised Land.
Plagues were quite common in Biblical days,
They came in tranches of seven,
And for many they were passports
To the Kingdom of Heaven!

But this Covid 19 is an exceptional case,
There is nothing to lend it an acceptable face.
It is silent, invisible, sudden, ruthless and cruel,
And it shows no respect for persons, religion or race.
It builds up momentum at a frightening pace.
There will be sudden loss of family and lovers.
And, to add to the terror, when we think it is over,
We are told we can never be certain or sure
That this ruthless killer
Won't come back for more!

Take care of yourselves. You've done nothing wrong.
We are all human beings and we all belong
To one great family called to be of one mind.
It's important to recognise we are called humankind.
And that kindness will see us strive and survive
And share with each other the joy of being alive.

Peace in Our Time

Today we came close to a lover's tiff,
Or something that's worse where it seems as if
You are teetering close to the edge of a cliff.
Below the sea is in torment and smashing the rocks
And it seems that the elements are running amok.
All nature is in turmoil and you're in total despair
Faced with the loss of a loving affair.
It could so easily have happened
But you remained calm
And took me to a place
That was safe,
Far away from all harm.

A Christmas Invitation (2003)

It's not exactly Bethlehem
With tents and inns and things;
There may be a few stables
But we don't expect three kings;
There may have been a census
Earlier this year
But it didn't mean
People had to flock
In winter or in fear.

But Thornton can still act as host
For the Saviour of mankind;
He can come down and dwell with us
If we seek then we shall find.
We'll greet him at our Christmas Mass
And make him feel at home,
Give Bethlehem a miss this year
Thornton's the place to come.

It's a peaceful place is Thornton
Near the sea and miles of beach
And places like the Lake District
All within easy reach.
There are horses, too, and lots of cows
And a river meandering by,
With seagulls swooping overhead
In a blue if wintry sky.

So come to Thornton, Jesus,
We'll make you feel at home.
And if you like it, as we're sure you will,
You will feel no need to roam.
We've a cosy little church here
(You know that Nicholas Owen)
And the folk who go, you'll also know,
Won't leave you all alone.
They'll visit you every day there
And have a little chat
And, even if it were Bethlehem,
You can't ask more than that!

Feet First

There is something quite erotic about podiatry
With its subtle hint of nudity.
Although, to be fair, there's nothing really shocking
About the removal of the client's stockings!
But how lovely is the soft caress
Of the feet. The excitement of flesh on flesh.
Some might say the sight of ugly corns and bunions
Would suggest lesions rather than liaisons.
The neglected toes and ingrown nails
Might well suggest all passion fails.
But love conquers all as all romantics know
That's how Juliet met her Romeo.
It had nothing to do with a squabble in the street:
She was a podiatrist
And he had trouble with his feet!

Repent at Leisure

We married, some have said, in some haste,
But, at the time, it seemed for the best.
We set off happily for our honeymoon
Staying the night in South Kensington,
Happy bride and happy groom.

It wasn't the Ritz nor was it the Palace
But it had been booked by my darling Wallace.
He'd said it was handy for Mass next morning.
Sadly, that had to be as the day was dawning,
Cos our boat was leaving for France at ten
And we hadn't much time to spare, y'ken.

The room he had booked was four floors high:
"This, is lovely, dear Wallace," (a little white lie)
"We'll be nearer the stars and the London night sky".
And I heaved up our suitcase which my Wallace had packed.
He's a love, dear thing, but he has a bad back.

We had eaten a hearty supper for two
Of bacon and eggs washed down with Irn Bru.
But, now we were tired and ready for bed
We'd had a long day and plenty of travel,
But that was when things began to unravel.

Being good Catholics this was the first time
I'd shared the same bedroom with this dear love of mine.
Imagine my horror as I saw him undress
I am certain you'll understand my distress.

First off came the leg (I thought he had two)
I never thought he'd one to unscrew!
Then off came that crowning glory – his hair-
Which he casually laid on the back of the chair!
Out came the teeth which I'd always admired.
Suddenly, I felt weak and so very tired.

"Come to bed, Wallace," I whispered in his ear
And suddenly found a hearing aid there.
"I'm coming, my darling, but you will need to shout
And I can't see a thing with my contact lens out."
Wallace stumbled and fell, then struck the bedpost!
Our night of romance was totally lost.

Friendship

I never thought the day would come
When I would say my greatest chum
Came in the shape of a frisky cockapoo
Well, let's be fair, would it happen to you?
I'm sure your reaction would be one of surprise.
You're bound to suggest, "Something's wrong with your eyes"
Or, "You've taken leave of your senses, come on, get a grip
You must be on something, on some kind of trip!"

But, in fact, I'm quite serious
I feel young at heart
And one thing is certain
All the dogs have played a great part
In bringing us together
Each day in the park
Where's there's nothing sweeter
Than the sound of their bark.
It tells of their joy and their happiness, too,
And the lovely new friendship between me and you.

L'Amour

Two lovers cling in close embrace
As they share their sweet kisses face to face
Completely oblivious of time and place.
Seeking to share the exquisite pleasure
That love-making can bring beyond all measure.
Of all life's experiences surely the treasure.
Whether it's midnight or mid-afternoon,
By the glare of the sun or the light of the moon,
Love-making days or nights of fierce passion
Will surely never go out of fashion.
And one word that all lovers hate and decry
Is that anarchic, unromantic aberration: GOODBYE.
It's so final, abrupt, holds no hope for the future,
Where *au revoir, a bientot, bonne nuit mon amour*,
Make all lovers feel much more safe and secure.

Con Amore

I Remember …

(An alternative approach to that of Thomas Hood)

I remember, I remember
The house where I was born
The windows there were never clean
And the curtains were all torn.
I was the family's middle child,
The middle one of seven,
But, when I was born, I'm sad to say,
My little sister, Kathleen,
Had already gone to heaven.
Which left just one little girl
My lovely sister, Joan,
Amongst those five unruly boys
She felt so all alone.

Our rented house was in Boreland Street
In Bootle, quite near the docks,
Its structure was quite primitive
The style: well …back to back!
If our house was rather crowded
So was the whole street, too,
There wasn't room to swing a cat
Though we probably swung a few!

But, in September 1939 we found a removal man
His name was Adolf Hitler and he didn't use a van!
He organised some aeroplanes to bombard Bootle docks,
By the time they had finished
Those houses had no need for locks!

But before our house had been bombed to bits
We'd been moved away from harm.
One kid I knew, who'd never seen a cow
Was evacuated to a farm.
We were rather luckier – evacuated to Southport—
Though, for some, pardon the pun,
It was the last resort!

We disembarked in Hillside – it has its own golf course—
This motley crew of waifs and strays tumbled off the bus.
Me and my brother, Lawrence, stood holding hands together,
We were at the seaside, we could even see the shore.
Imagine how we felt that day, two small evacuees,
A kindly lady saw me: "I'd like to take that one, please."
The evacuations officer, I'm glad to say, came to my rescue,
"You're not allowed to split them up – you have to take the two!"

And that, indeed, is what she did:
She walked us to her house:
The cleanest house I'd ever seen
Not a sign of a mouse or a louse!!
The sun shone through the windows
There were pictures on the walls
There were carpets instead of lino
Not like Boreland Street at all.

But Lol and I did not stay long
Perhaps our Scouse accents were too strong.
He went one way, I went the other,
How I missed my younger brother.
The family that Lol went to treated him so badly,
Whilst I was loved and welcomed by the kindly Marshall family.

After a year, at last, the Hylands all got together.
This time, Old Alf, the undertaker, was the lucky fella!
His job had saved him from armed combat, from fighting in the war,
He thought he had been lucky, now he was not so sure!
We played among the coffins, we created so much noise,
Alf was used to dealing with the dead
Now there were five lively Bootle boys!

We stayed with Alf for two long years.
But then in '43
We were moved to 34 Bedford Road,
And set poor Alfie free!
The house had no electricity
It had gas for cooking and light.
It had no indoor plumbing
We had a tin bath on Saturday night.
If we wanted to go to the toilet
There was a privy at the end of the yard,
It was smelly, and right next to the coal hole,
O, life as a boy, was so hard!

Long after the war the family all went our separate ways:
Two went to Australia, two to Varsity,
One went down South, the other went to the far north-west.
Dad died when he was 54; at 84 Mum went to her rest.
We now all had clean windows, and life's other better things.
But there is no way of escaping those curtains
That the end of our life brings.

A Christmas Sceptic

The queues at the Post Office are now seven deep
They've few stamps left for the demands are steep.
Ancient customers begin to moan-
It's been hours since they left their home –
"Where are we?" one is heard to say,
"I've only come here to get my pension.
But, with these long queues I think the tension.
Will prove too much, and I'll spend Christmas
In a hospital bed!"
Which, having said,
He sank to his knees
Holding his head.
But, this is the season of good will to all men
So, people rushed to his side to offer him help.
But, as he got to his feet, he let out a yelp:
"My pension book's gone and so is my wallet!
I bet one of you b*****s has helped himself to it!
Just get your hands off me and leave me alone.
I've still got my bus pass, I'll find my way home."

It's a tale with a moral – I'm sure it has –
It must tell us something about the advent of Christmas.
Perhaps the commotion I've just described here
Makes us all grateful it's just once a year!

Victory In Europe

The year was 1945
And I was lucky to be alive.
I had short trousers
And a snotty nose then,
A scruffy Scouser
Who had just turned ten.
We'd been bombed out of Bootle
When I was just four
My first introduction to what they called WAR.
What happened in the next six years
Is too painful to relate.
I can tell you there were lots of tears
But not much food upon the plate!
However, on that sunny day on Tuesday 8th of May
We celebrated joyfully the first Victory in Europe Day!
The streets were decked with Union Jacks
There were trestle tables all well stacked
With whatever folk could find to eat
ANYTHING WITH JAM WOULD BE A TREAT!
All washed down with fizzy pop.
And people danced till fit to drop.
I joined my pals on the back of a truck.
We had flags to wave and we shouted "Good luck"
To everybody we passed on the way
Celebrating victory on that 8th of May.
And 75 years later here we all are
Reminding ourselves we had won a World War.
Each house had a table filled with all kinds of treats
Wine, whisky, tequila stretched right down the street.
There was music and flags, banners, bunting and singing
There's no holds barred when you celebrate winning!
The sky was resplendent, the sun was aglow
Those 75 years... O where did they go?

Away In A Manger

In many a draughty village hall
Fond parents are gathered, one and all,
To see a familiar story played:
A baby in a manger laid.

There they see familiar sights:
Laundered tea-towels (preferably striped)
Barely concealing a loved child's face,
Whilst shepherds wander all over the place!

No missing Mary – she's in blue-
But Joseph, type-cast, has just one thing to do:
He's got to find a room at the inn
And meets a young inn-keeper
Who can't help but grin.

"My wife and I have nowhere to stay,
We've not been able to come till today.
We've been doing our shopping and are proper worn out,
Please say you've a room, don't say you've nowt."

The little inn-keeper gave a broad smile
He'd been waiting for this moment for quite a while
Until now he'd never been able
To offer a couple a place in his stable.

"I'm sure you'll be very comfortable here,
It's really quite warm for this time of year,
The breath of the animals might get up your nose
But that's the least of your troubles, I suppose."

Inside the stable there were animals galore:
There were penguins and zebras and lions that roar,
The teacher had made sure that all had a part
She was looking quite anxious right from the start.

Then a small, squeaky recorder is heard
Played by a shepherd with an unusual beard,
Hooked over one ear and not the other,
A child in the audience cries: "That's my brother!"

There's hardly a dry eye in the village hall
At what has happened in a humble stall,
The birth of a baby brings so much joy
Especially the birth of this little Boy.

Christmas

Crackers and candles and cattle in stalls
Heavenly angels singing hallelujahs
Robins and reindeer and Rudolph, of course,
Icicles clinging to old stone walls
Santa has called and left all the toys
This, after all, is the Season of Joys.
My hope for you is that all will be well
And that you and your loved ones enjoy this Noel.
So may it be. Alleluia. Amen

Twenty Twenty Two

New Year Resolutions

1. I must be sure to have a daily shower,
   I know of some who stay by the hour.
   But having a shower to open the day
   Could serve as my 2022 cachet.

2. I must improve on my driving performance,
   At present I drive as though in a trance.
   I must concentrate more, respect other road users,
   I could finish the year with fewer abusers.

3. I must make more effort to be less fussy:
   Eat what I'm given, even if I feel queasy.
   Retrain my taste buds to accept new tastes,
   I will feel so much fuller and bring an end to food waste.

4. I must get used to these hearing aids,
   Especially when you think what the NHS paid
   To stop me saying, "Sorry. What did you say?"
   I'll lose lots of friends if I go on that way.

5. One thing to improve on is visiting friends
   Which I used to be good at but now tends
   To be rarer than it ever has been.
   I will make every effort to be back on the scene.

6. One fault that I have that makes people bristle
   Is when I start humming or, even worse, whistle.
   I don't know how I developed that habit
   But it's finished, I promise. If you hear it, shout "STOP IT".

FINALLY:
I hope the New Year brings you contentment,
Is free of any form of resentment,
Brings you peace of mind, free of stress,
Safe from all harm, full of happiness.

HAPPY NEW YEAR

Le Mariage

The wedding venue was in Le Canon
On the south-west coast of France.
But this was no shot-gun wedding
Simply nothing was left to chance.
Le Canon borders the ocean
There are yachts bobbing in the bay.
If you want a taste of heaven on earth
Go there on a summer's day.
The sea is a rich translucent blue
Reflecting the sky above.
It's the perfect place for a marriage,
It's where people fall in love.

The preparation for the wedding
Was a logistics *tour de force*:
The sea-walls around the lawn's edging
Had to be painted – green and white, of course –
And wooden flooring covered everything in sight,
To provide space for the dancing on the happy night.
Great tables were erected that spread from east to west
As the banquet for the wedding was for one hundred and twenty guests!
However, the *piece de resistance*, the peak of a host of delights
Came in the shape of magnificent tents, a glimpse of Arabian Nights!

The wedding itself took place out of doors
On a jetty abutting the sea.
The water sparkled, scintillating, sublime –
It was like an Impressionist painting
Caught for ever in a moment of time.
And yet, that study in beauty
Was outdone by the guests on the shore –
Be amazed – hold your breath – stand in awe!

There were photos galore that were taken that day
And the professional captured the dazzling array
Of beauty and glamour and startling creations-
It was the stuff of dreams and wild imagination.
There were so many stunning damsels of amazing *eclat*
Including show-stopping Mama in her wonderful hat.
And, as for the men, they were a joy to behold:
Well-groomed, and well-suited, doing what they were told!

And so, *enfin*, the scene was set,
And, to the strains of an instrumental duet,
A vision in white came into view,
And a fairy-tale dream was about to come true.
Vows of love and fidelity were sealed with a kiss:
There is nothing in life quite as beautiful as this.

It was the French who first said "joie de vivre "
And Hollywood brought us "Saturday Night Fever "
They both came together in dining and dancing
And, without doubt, a fair share of romancing!
There's no doubt le diner was all cordon bleu,
The wine flowed in abundance – well we were in Bordeaux!
Nineteen nationalities filled the tables that night
But all could speak English so that was alright!

So, we wined and we dined
And "set the table on a Roar "
Time to work off some calories
Time to dance on that floor!
But this was not "keep fit," this time
It was time for romance
As the newly wed couple
Stepped forward for the dance.
They were a thing of beauty
The quintessence of all charms,
As they swayed beneath a starry sky
Wrapped in each other's arms.

May the memory of that wondrous day
Linger ever in their mind
When everything was beautiful
And everyone was kind.

It was a day so full of colour
It was a day so full of love.
So dear Bride and dear Groom
Wherever you may rove,
May the years that stretch before you
Become a treasure trove.

"Come live with me and be my love"

Note: *There is a famous 16th century poem with this line written by Christopher Marlowe. He also wrote the play Doctor Faustus the man who sold his soul to the devil! Marlowe himself was killed in a fight in a tavern! What follows is a terrible parody of Marlowe's lovely poem!*

Come live with me and be my love
And life will be a treasure trove.
I'd shower so many kisses on you
You'd feel the earth beneath you move!
I'd hang upon your every word
I'd anticipate all your wishes,
I'd use the vacuum every day
I'd wash up all the dishes!
You could watch whatever TV you liked
Even Coronation Street,
I'd buy a bag of candy
You could choose your favourite sweet!
I'd take my dirty shoes off when I came into the house,
I'd put my new, nice slippers on,
I'd be as quiet as a mouse.
If there is anything else you would like me to do
Just say the word,
No matter how absurd
I would do anything for you.

November

Prompted by Thomas Hood's poem of the same name!

No more basking in warm weather
No more willow on red leather
No more punting on the river
No more blue skies – no, not ever –
No more girls in scanty clothing
No more nudists wearing nothing!
No more shapely tennis players
No more sensual sun-bathers
No more surfing or even paddling
No more outdoor amorous cuddling
No more flowers bombarded by bees
No more gardens or luxuriant trees
No more songbirds or butterflies
No more tastes of paradise
No more joys can we remember
No more ... no more ... no more ...
NOVEMBER

Ode to 'Alifax

In the days of steam
When aspirates were ignored
'"Ull', Elland , 'Alifax"'
The platform guard would roar.
To the uninitiated traveller
It conjured up fear and dread
At the prospect of destinations
Filled with pain and death ahead.
But times have changed as you'd expect
We now pronounce our 'aitches'
And we celebrate with due respect
These towns noted now for ages.

What follows here are some of the tracks
That took us both round Halifax:
The first of note was Gibbet Street
Where life and death together meet.
There, many a so-called villain met
His sorry end as he paid his debt.
His head would be separated from his body
His dying word was probably 'Sorry!'
There's a certain balance in this story
Which is certainly gruesome and a little gory.
For the patron saint of Halifax
Also lost his head thanks to an axe!
Poor John the Baptist met his fate
And had his head delivered on a plate!
You will find his image on the wonderful gate
Which leads you into the Piece Hall.

This is now an elegant shopping mall
A beautiful conversion of an historic gem
Rooted in Yorkshire history when
Cloth was at the heart of Yorkshire trade
And weavers brought the cloth they made
To have its quality surveyed.

Another Halifax industry
Were the carpets produced by John Crossley
A gigantic business in the eighteenth century.
John Crossley built a Model Village
With dwellings of Gothic vintage
To provide superb dwellings for his workers!
It's a glorious testimony not to be missed
A credit to a Yorkshire philanthropist.

Another outstanding Yorkshire figure
Was the noted lesbian Anne Lister
Who is celebrated now as Gentlemen Jack.
She owned a coalmine and always dressed in black!
This wealthy woman owned Shibden Hall –
A magnificent place well worth a visit
Though, as a travelling woman she was rarely in it!

Halifax is graced by green oases.
It's full of parks and splendid places
Like Halifax Minster and Crossley's Mausoleum,
Take time to saunter – you will really like them-
"Nisi Dominus custodierit civitatem"
Is Halifax's Latin motto.
Which loosely translated means "The Lord's the one to go to"
Literally: "Unless the Lord protects the city"—
(It will go to hell and that would be a pity!)

It seems to me that our last port of call
Was the most important site of all.
For it was in Elland that Pamela spent many a year
And it was fitting that we should linger here.
Make no mistake, you can be sure,
This was the highlight of our tour.

Christmas 2018

Some don't believe in Christmas
And all that stuff about a stall
And angels, shepherds, and oxen
And virgin births and all.
They say it's all a fairy tale
Or even worse, a fantastic fib
Told by a Mary, young and pale,
And all for a bit part in a crib!

But there was a Jesus Christ all right
Born, no doubt, on a starry night,
And, like many birth chronicles of ancient men,
The write-ups could be quite startling when
They proved later to be great successes –
At times, those histories could be inspired guesses.

So, let's enjoy this lovely Feast,
If nothing else we can say at least
That it makes December a little more cheery
I do hope for you it proves to be MERRY.

Rain Stopped Play

At last! The sound of mallet on missile
An act of aggression not seen for a while.
That real sense of power, of control and possession
In an arena where there's credit for unfettered aggression.
Where each player is invited to choose their best weapon
And wreak havoc and confusion with no hint of compunction.
For weeks now we've suffered from unceasing rain
We thought we'd never play croquet again.
The Park was awash – a muddy terrain.
We waited for the sun but waited in vain .
We fretted and frowned, we vented our spleens
Grown men shed tears, there were terrible scenes
As they suddenly felt like worthless has-beens.
The ladies, of course, were much better controlled
They were patient, long suffering (or so I was told)
They knew it would pass, we would come through the crisis
We'd be better and stronger after ordeals just like this.
And that is what happened – we are together again
Swinging our mallets with no hint of restraint.

Your Valentine

It is surely not just by chance
That the loving feeling known as 'Romance'
Has a distinctly Italian ring
For the whole Valentine thing
Can surely be traced back to Rome
As you will find as you read this poem!
It was always taken as a 'given'
That the best fighting men
Would not be saddled with a woman.
A soldier is single-minded
And is certainly not blinded
By feelings of love and compassion.
He must kill and be ready to take a life
There's no room in that philosophy for a wife!
Now Valentine was a Catholic priest
And took quite another view.
He married soldiers in secrecy
And believe me there were quite a few.
When this was discovered
He was flung into jail.
His pleas for mercy were to no avail.
There is a happy ending despite this disaster
For the priest developed feelings for the gaoler's daughter!
I wish I could say they lived happily ever after.
But it is from one of his many letters
That we have that immortal line
Which lovers often write:
" I am your Valentine."

I Love You

I love you as I love the calm
Of sweet, star-spangled hours,
I love you as I love the balm
Of early jasmine flowers.

I love you as I love the last
Rich smile of a fading day
Which lingers like the look we shared
On our magical first day.

I love you as I love the tune
Of a mellow saxophone
Which plays a melody I've chosen
Just for you alone.

I love you as I love the first
Young violets of Spring
Or the daffodils fresh sprung from earth
And proudly blossoming.

I love you as I love the full
Clear burst of a thrush's song.
That melody so rich and sweet
Tells of the way I long
To be with you and speak with you
And hold you in my arms
And share with you for all my life
Your beauty and your charms.

When we are old and grey and full of sleep

When we are old and grey and full of sleep
And, nodding by the fire, look back at life,
Remember that fine day in summer's heat
When I first asked you to be my wife.

Like many more I loved your lovely face
The smile that set the room alight
The lilting voice that had such style and grace
The tinkling laughter echoing your delight.

Remember then how deep in love we were
The agony of being far apart
The need to be together where
We could feel the beating of each other's heart.

Then as we huddle close to the dying embers of the fire
And watch the coals grow colder
Thank God our love has grown
And never lost its warmth
As we grow older.

You Are Lovely

When I hear you say "You're lovely"
I know for sure that you're sincere
I know it's not some tired cliché
Just something you know I'd like to hear.
For I can see the sweetest smile
I can see those eyes that shine
And I have known now for a while
That I am yours and you are mine.
And when I say 'I think you're lovely'
I'm not serving as an echo
I'm saying I'm so glad you love me
I'm saying that I love you, too.

So, what is it that so attracts me ?
What is it that makes me feel
That you and I were meant to be?
What is the secret of your appeal?
There is, of course, your natural beauty
And add to this your joie de vivre
I love the smiles with which you greet me
And I feel the grief when you have to leave.
I love the music of your laughter
The sharing of our memories
And I think that ever after
We can add many more of these.

Advice on the Onset of Old Age

(prompted by a 17th century poem by Thomas Vaux)

I've just looked in the mirror and got a fright
Those raven locks have turned to white!
And, o dear me, they've gone quite scarce,
Things are going from bad to worse.

What consolation can be had, I wonder.
Give me a second ... I must ponder.
Perhaps it's time to call it a day,
Admit I'm old and it's time to pray.
See these white hairs as warning signs,
Time to say sorry for all those times
I failed to be all that I should
Times when I was naughty and ought to have been good!

Those wrinkles and that balding top
Suggest it's time I called a stop
To all those shenanigans and gallivantings
And focused on more serious things.
The time is nigh ... it may be nigher,
Send in that application for the celestial choir!
Bend those knees, join those hands,
It's time to get ready for the heavenly bands ...

                                        Amen, Man!

Christmas Din Din

We love the sounds of Christmas
Like the jingle of the tills
Like Santa calling Ho-Ho-Ho
Or the chime of Christmas bells.
The sounding of the merry organ,
Sweet singing in the choir,
The murmur of a church at prayer
At the magic midnight hour.
The delighted sounds of children
As they open Christmas toys,
The popping of the champagne corks
And lots of other noise.
But the sound that offsets all such din
Is when Mum brings the dinner in,
For that's when Dad lets out that shout
'Go easy with those lethal sprouts!'
Spare a thought for this humble vegetable
Who's rarely welcome at the Christmas table,
Most meet their end by being binned
Whilst others pass away as wind!

Boy Meets Girl

I was always awkward and terribly shy
When it came to talking to girls.
I have never really quite understood why
My mind seemed to spin and to whirl.
Perhaps, if my mother had given me more hints
Or my father been a little more frank
I'd have had more success and not hidden so much
My experience with girls was a blank.

But then I met you, and my heart took a leap,
I knew, from the moment we met,
That my life up till then had no beauty or joy
That a boy needs a girl and a girl needs a boy
That I was to be yours and you were to be mine
I will love you for ever my sweet Valentine.

Victorian Values

"Tempus Edax Rerum"
O how the Victorians
Liked to scare 'em!
With thoughts of death
And, of course, damnation
Such thoughts helped shape
An obedient nation.
O, yes, we said
That Britain was great
But it also engendered
Fiercesome hate
As it built an empire
Based on slaves
With its mighty warships –
Britannia ruled the waves.

But Britain also
Waived the rules
Or invented some
For those regarded as fools –
The neglected, downtrodden and indigent poor,
With lives blighted by bosses
Whose motto was:
MORE!

So, when you see
A Victorian monument,
With its grey or black marble
And serious intent,
Note how grim and hard
Brutal, severe and forbidding
More concerned for the dead
Than for the living
And demanding attention
Tenets that helped forge
A submissive nation.
"Time devours things"
As the Latin translates,
But also devours people
Who are summoned to Death
By the discordant bells of a grim church steeple.

The End of Friendship

Goodness knows how often the case has been made
Over and over but to deaf ears I'm afraid,
About English spelling and its irregular behaviour
It's about time spelling experts did us a favour
And not leave us all so confused and dumbfounded!
One example of this is the spelling of 'friendship'
Where the first of the 'i's' is clearly redundant
And could make English learners utterly despondent.
But the philosophers' angle is relevant here
For they argue that the 'I' is the intruder to fear
If the 'I' is conspicuous in any relationship
If the 'I' seeks to dominate it will threaten the partnership
So cut out the 'i', bring it painlessly to an end,
And just get used to having a frend!

The LFC Victory Parade

We were runners-up, we were also-rans,
We were second-best, disappointed all our fans.
We'd built up their hopes, promised the best,
We'd won two trophies and wanted the rest.
But it all came to nought, our hopes simply collapsed,
The burning Ring of Fire crumbled to ash.
And yet, within twenty-four hours we had the Victory Parade!
For the Boys on the Bus it was not a charade.
They showed their delight at what they had won:
Two cups in one season should please anyone.
The two trophies sparkled in the Merseyside sun!
So, be of good spirits, keep that cheeky Scouse smile,
We've won two shining trophies and done it in style.
We'll have a new stand at the Anfield Road end,
Just think of the message that will send!
"We're back and we're ready, this is a war zone,
We are Liverpool and we never walk alone!"

When I'm Gone ... An Obituary Piece

Please mourn for me when I've passed on
Be sad, forlorn, be woe-begone
For I have loved this life so much:
The joy of music, a loving touch,
The beauty of flowers, the songs of birds,
The delight of colour, the magic of words,
The laughter of friends, the love of family, such things have
    meant so much to me.
That sense of bliss
I always found at the exchange of a kiss
I cannot imagine anything better than this.
My faith assures me there is another life
And I have always clung to this belief.
So pray that all I believed was true
And, if I am in Heaven, I will pray for you.

Illustrations

Front cover and page 73	Linear graphic adaption by Bryan Trueman of a donkey at Blackpool seafront from an original photograph by Peter Brennan.
Page iv	Original photograph of deckchairs on the Pier at Blackpool by Peter Brennan.
Page vii	Original photograph of dancing couple at the Tower Ballroom in Blackpool by Peter Brennan.
Page 5	Original graphic of "The Fantasy Marathon" by Bryan Trueman incorporating photographic images of both Sally Ford , marathon runner and holder of a Guinness World Record and Bryan Trueman.
Page 22	Original graphic of "the Hit and Run Disaster … 2006" by Bryan Trueman.
Page 35	Original graphic of "Valentine" by Bryan Trueman.
Page 53	Photograph of Bootle, Liverpool (photographer unknown), showing wartime bomb damage courtesy of Sefton War Memorials at Sefton Library Service with additional photographic images incorporated by Bryan Trueman comprising two young boys (courtesy of Alamy) and the author as a young boy (photographer unknown).
Page 83	Linear graphic adaption by Bryan Trueman of the Wurlitzer (courtesy of the Phil Kelsall website).
Page 87	Original photograph of a donkey at Blackpool seafront by Peter Bremon.
Back cover	Original photograph of the Author by Pamela Norrington.

About:

Peter Brennan is an established professional Australian photographer who lives in Sydney, NSW. Peter specialises in urban landscapes and his clients include both private individuals and commercial organisations .

Bryan Trueman is an English artist, printmaker and ceramicist with a successful international career in Australia, the US and the UK. Now settled in Suffolk, England, Bryan continues to create and exhibit his artwork .

www.ingramcontent.com/pod-product-compliance
Lightning Source LLC
LaVergne TN
LVHW041634070426
835507LV00008B/608